Table of Contents

Your Reward	6
Introduction	7
Author's Note	8
All About Maple Syrup	9
What is Maple Syrup?	9
How is Maple Syrup Made?	9
Where is Maple Syrup Produced?	10
How was Maple Syrup Discovered?	10
Can Maple Syrup be Substituted for Sugar in Recipes?	11
Is Maple Syrup a Healthy Choice?	11
Maple Syrup Fun Facts	12
The Syrup Used for the Recipes in this Book	13
The Recipes	
BREAKFAST	14
Maple Monkey Bread	15
Maple Candied Bacon	16
Maple Bran Muffins	17
Blueberry Maple Breakfast Bread Pudding	18
Maple Scones	19
LUNCH	21
Monte Cristo Sandwich with Maple Syrup Dip	22
Spinach, Quinoa & Pear Salad with Maple Vinaigrette	24
Maple Curried Red Lentil Soup	26
Maple and Sriracha Chicken Wings	28
SNACKS	30
Maple Bacon Party Mix	31
Maple Spiced Candied Nuts	32

DINNER 33
- Roasted Lemon-Maple Chicken 34
- Sesame and Maple Crusted Lamb Chops 36
- Maple, Ale & Garlic Pork Shoulder 37
- Maple-Cardamom Glazed Salmon 39
- Maple Garlic Dijon Chicken 40
- Maple Vegetable Enchiladas 41
- Maple Mustard Pork Tenderloin 44
- Slow Cooker Maple Ham 46
- Maple-Pistachio Seared Scallops 47
- SIDE DISHES 48
- Brussels Sprouts & Carrots with Maple Syrup 49
- Maple -Apple Rice 50
- Maple Mashed Sweet Potatoes 51
- DESSERT 52
- Maple Almond Squares 53
- Maple Apple Pie 55
- Peach Crisp with Maple Cream Sauce 57
- Bourbon Maple Bacon and Pecan Cookies 59
- Maple Syrup Gingerbread Cookies 61
- Maple Panna Cotta 63
- Sweet & Spicy Nutty Maple Bites 64
- Nutmeg-Maple Cream Pie 66

BREAD 68
- Maple Syrup Raisin Bread 69
- Sweet Potato Maple Beer Bread 70

Maple-Lemon Zucchini Bread	72
Sour Cream-Maple Bread	74
Maple White Bread	75
Maple Syrup Corn Bread	77
COCKTAILS	79
The Bubbly Maple Leaf	80
The Maple Bourbon Twist	81
Rum & Maple with Lime	82
Bonus Recipe	83
About the Author	85
A Request	87

A Gift for You

To say "Thank You" for buying *The Maple Syrup Cookbook,* we'd like to give you a copy of *Favorite Recipes*, a collection of 18 recipes for delicious and easy-to-prepare dishes from appetizers to baked goods to entrées to desserts.

Get Your Free Copy Here:
http://www.fastforwardpublishing.com/Thank-You-Favorite-Recipes.html

Introduction

Welcome to my second volume of Maple Syrup recipes. The recipes are different, but the Maple Syrup "story" has stayed same. So, instead of writing a new introduction and informational segments in the beginning of this book, I'm using the same information from the first book. If you have the first book, you're just coming here for the recipes anyway, so skip ahead. If you're new to exploring the culinary appeal of Maple Syrup, enjoy this overview.

Professional chefs and home cooks are discovering the taste and benefits of Maple Syrup beyond its traditional place in desserts and at the breakfast table. Used with a variety ingredients in a full list of cooking Instructions and styles, Maple Syrup is showing up as an ingredient in meals from lunch to dinner and from snacks to drinks.
beyond its traditional place in desserts and at the breakfast table. Used with a variety ingredients in a full list of cooking Instructions and styles, Maple Syrup is showing up as an ingredient in meals from lunch to dinner and from snacks to drinks.

For everyone -- from omnivore to vegan -- Maple Syrup offers a healthy alternative to sugar while imparting a pleasingly unique flavor to meals all around the world. I hope you enjoy this sampling of the exciting recipes that we have put together for this book.

Author's Note

I recently enjoyed an extended stay in Burlington, Vermont where Maple Syrup is a tradition that some Vermonters say is in their blood. They take their Maple Syrup seriously in Vermont and I feasted on many culinary offerings featuring that sweet, golden liquid treasure. Along with my childhood memories of Maple Syrup on pancakes and oatmeal, this visit inspired the writing of this book.

Every producer will vigorously defend his locale as the epicenter of Maple Syrup excellence. I'm not going to weigh in on who produces the best syrup (or maple sugar, or maple butter, or maple candy, etc.), but I will state that, for most purposes, I prefer the medium or dark amber Maple Syrup over the light amber. I guess that, in regards to Maple Syrup, I'm a grade B kind of guy. And, so as not to foment conflict between countries and states, regions and cities, towns and sugarhouses, that's as far as I'm willing to go in stating any kind of preference in regards to Maple Syrup.

All About Maple Syrup

What is Maple Syrup?

Maple syrup comes from the sap of maple trees. In the early spring, if you cut the bark or drill a hole into some species of maple trees, thin, clear sap (almost like water) will leak from the cut. This sap is about 2-percent sucrose and when boiled, the water evaporates, leaving maple syrup.

NOTE: Although some people tap the red maple and the silver maple, most will agree that the sap of the sugar (or rock) maple and the black maple produce the best syrup.

How is Maple Syrup Made?

When the sap of the maple tree flows in the late winter and early spring, it is collected for syrup making.

NOTE: Sap collection is best on days when the temperature is above freezing during the day and below freezing at night prior to bud formation. After the trees start to bud and produce leaves, the quality of the sap dramatically changes and cannot be used to produce syrup.

In the old days, a hole was drilled in the maple tree and a spout-like tap called a spile was inserted into the hole and a bucket was placed below the spile to collect the sap. These days, the sap is collected through plastic tubing

Once the sap has been collected, it is boiled down for hours in a special evaporator while it is monitored for viscosity and sugar density. Once boiled down, the syrup is filtered, graded and hot-packed (into sterile containers in a hot water bath).

Pure maple syrup is sold by shades of "amber." Although there are some different standards between states and countries that produce maple syrup, typically:

Light Amber has a fine, delicate flavor.
Medium Amber has a richer flavor and is most frequently used as table syrup.
Dark Amber is used for cooking, or as a table syrup by those who prefer a strong maple flavor.

Where is Maple Syrup Produced?

Because of specific weather conditions, maple syrup is only produced in the Northern part of North America, primarily in Quebec and Ontario in Canada and Maine, Massachusetts, Michigan, New Hampshire, New York, Ohio, Pennsylvania, Vermont, and Wisconsin in the United States.

NOTE: Quebec produces about three-quarters of the world's output

How Was Maple Syrup Discovered?

According to legend, one late-winter morning, Iroquois Chief Woksis, on his way to go hunting, pulled his tomahawk from the tree where he'd thrown it the night before. The weather was unseasonably warm and the tree's sap dripped from the gash made from the tomahawk and filled a container that was standing near the trunk. When the Chief's wife walked by the tree later, she thought container was plain water and cooked their evening meal in it. When boiled, the sap turned to syrup and the Chief liked the flavor. From that meal on, the Iroquois made and taught others to make maple syrup.

Can Maple Syrup be Substituted for Sugar in Recipes?

As a general rule of thumb, you can substitute one cup of maple granulated sugar for one cup of white sugar. Or, you can use one cup of maple syrup, but you'll also want to reduce any liquids in the recipe by approximately 3.7 ounces (between ⅓ cup and ½ cup) for each cup of sugar replaced.

NOTE: According to researchers at the International Maple Syrup Institute pure maple syrup delivers more overall nutritional value than many common sweeteners and has one of the lowest calorie levels while providing enhanced antioxidant levels. It may contain other health benefits that are currently being studied.

Is Maple Syrup a Healthy Choice?

When choosing between traditional sweeteners, pure Maple Syrup is a healthy option. Along with its sweetness and signature flavor, it also delivers beneficial vitamins, minerals and antioxidants.

Nutritional Value for Various Sweeteners
% of Recommended Daily Value (DV) per ¼ cup (60 ml)

	Maple Syrup	Corn Syrup	Honey	Brown Sugar	White Sugar
Manganese	95	0	4	2	0
Riboflavin	37	1	2	0	1
Zink	6	0	2	0	0
Magnesium	7	0	1	2	0
Calcium	5	0	0	4	0
Potassium	5	0	1	1	0
Calories	216	220	261	216	196

SOURCE: Canadian Nutrient File (Health Canada) and USDA Nutrient Database

Pure maple syrup is also very rich in antioxidants. It is reported that maple syrup has over 54 antioxidants that can help delay or prevent diseases caused by free radicals. The USDA database lists pure maple syrup on par or better than many vegetables when it comes to their antioxidant values.

Maple Syrup is also low on the Glycemic Index weighing in at (54) while white sugar is at (58) and honey is at (87). Expert agree that by consuming foods (55) or lower on the Glycemic Index can potentially help prevent or control diabetes, heart disease, and obesity.

Fun Facts About Maple Syrup

- It takes 30-50 gallons of sap to make one gallon of maple syrup.

- A maple that produces sap that can be made into maple sugar is called a sugarmaple.

- An area with a high concentration of sugarmaples is called a sugarbush.

- The building in which the maple syrup is produced is called a sugarhouse.

- The person who makes the maple syrup is called a sugarmaker.

- Native Americans were the first sugarmakers and they taught the Europeans all about the process.

- Maple syrup is boiled even further to produce maple cream, maple sugar, and maple candy.

- It takes one gallon of maple syrup to produce eight pounds of maple candy or sugar.

- A gallon of maple syrup weighs 11 pounds.

- The sugar content of sap averages 2.5 percent; sugar content of maple syrup is at 66 percent or more.

- Usually a maple tree is at least 30 years old and 12 inches in diameter before it is tapped.

- Tapping does no permanent damage and only 10 percent of the tree's sap is collected each year.

- Many maple trees have been tapped for 150 or more years.

- As the tree increases in diameter, more taps can be added - up to a maximum of four taps.

- Each tap will yield an average of 10 gallons of sap per season.

- The maple season may last eight to ten weeks, but sap flow is heaviest for about 10-20 days in the early spring (when the temperature is above freezing during the day and below freezing at night prior to bud formation).

The Syrup Used for the Recipes in this Book

All the recipes in this book use pure maple syrup: maple sap that has been collected and boiled down to obtain pure syrup without chemical agents or preservatives.

Do not confuse real maple syrup with "maple-flavored" syrups (also referred to as "pancake syrup", "waffle syrup", "table syrup", etc.) which are typically flavored high fructose corn syrup.

Maple Monkey Bread

12 Servings

INGREDIENTS:

    2 cans/tubes (approx. 16 ounces each) uncooked refrigerated biscuits

    ½ cup granulated maple sugar

    1 teaspoon cinnamon

    ¾ cup butter, melted

    ½ cup maple syrup

INSTRUCTIONS:

1. Preheat oven to 350°F
2. Spray a 10" Bundt pan liberally with non-stick cooking spray
3. In a shallow bowl, combine the maple sugar and the cinnamon
4. Remove the biscuits from their packaging and cut them into quarters
5. Dip each biscuit quarter in melted butter and then roll it in the maple sugar/cinnamon mixture
6. Once dipped and rolled, place the biscuit quarter into the prepared Bundt pan
7. Combine the remaining butter with the maple syrup and pour the mixture over top of the biscuit quarters in the Bundt pan
8. Transfer the filled Bundt pan to the center rack of the oven and bake at 350°F until golden brown and no longer doughy in center. (about 28-32 minutes) Keep an eye on this dish as it cooks, you do not want to overcook or scorch it
9. When the monkey bread is properly cooked, remove it from the oven and allow it to cool in the pan for 10 minutes
10. When cooled, invert the Bundt pan on a serving plate and serve immediately, letting guests serve themselves by pulling off the easy-to-break-away pieces

Maple Candied Bacon

4 servings

INGREDIENTS:

    1 pound bacon, thick sliced

    ½ cup maple syrup

DIRECTIONS:

1. Preheat oven to 400°F
2. Line a rimmed baking sheet with foil
3. Put a baking rack on the foil-lined baking sheet
4. Drizzle the bacon slices with about ½ of the maple syrup
5. Transfer the sheet pan with the rack and bacon to the oven and bake at 400°F for 10-12 minutes
6. After baking for 10-12 minutes, gently flip each slice of bacon and drizzle the remaining maple syrup over them evenly
7. Bake at 400° F for a additional 5-10 minutes (depending on your desired level of crispness)
8. Remove the sheet/rack from the oven and let the bacon rest on the rack for 5 minutes
9. Transfer the bacon to a plate (not a paper towel) and serve (it will be a bit sticky)

    NOTE: you can follow this recipe, eliminating the rack, but the bacon will be very, very sticky

Maple Bran Muffins

12 servings

INGREDIENTS:

1 cup sour cream

⅔ cup maple syrup

3 eggs, beaten

1 cup all-purpose flour

1 cup bran

1 teaspoon baking powder

½ teaspoon baking soda

½ cup raisins

½ cup chopped walnuts

INSTRUCTIONS:

1. Preheat the oven to 350°F
2. Grease a 12 cup muffin tin
3. In a medium mixing bowl, whisk together the sour cream, maple syrup and eggs
4. In a large mixing bowl, combine the flour, bran, baking powder and baking soda
5. Add the sour cream/maple/egg mixture to the flour/bran mixture and mix quickly
6. Pour the batter evenly into the prepared muffin tins
7. Transfer the filled muffin tin to the middle shelf of the oven and bake at 350°F until a toothpick inserted into the center of one of the muffins comes out clean (about 20 minutes)
8. When the muffins are done, remove the muffin tin from the oven and allow the muffins to cool in the tin for 5 minutes before serving

Blueberry Maple Breakfast Bread Pudding

10 servings

INGREDIENTS:

    1 loaf of white bread, crusts removed, cut into 1-inch pieces

    4 ounces of cream cheese, cut into small cubes

    2 cups fresh blueberries, divided (can use frozen, but thaw first and drain thoroughly)

    8 eggs, beaten

    1½ cups milk

    ¼ cup butter, melted

    ¼ cup maple syrup plus more for serving

INSTRUCTIONS:

1. Preheat oven to 350° F
2. Grease an 8-inch square baking dish
3. Place half of the bread cubes in the prepared dish
4. Distribute the cream cheese cubes and half of the blueberries evenly over the bread
5. Cover the cream cheese and blueberries with the remaining bread cubes and blueberries
6. In a mixing bowl, whisk together the eggs, milk, maple syrup and butter
7. Pour the egg/milk/maple/butter over the bread mixture in the 8-inch baking dish
8. Transfer the filled baking dish to the center rack of the oven and bake at 350° F until a knife inserted in the center comes out clean (about 1 hour)
9. When the bread pudding is finished cooking, remove it from the oven and let it stand for 10 minutes
10. Cut the bread pudding into squares and serve with additional maple syrup

Maple Scones

12 servings

INGREDIENTS:

    3 cups all-purpose flour

    1½ Tablespoons baking powder

    ¾ teaspoon Kosher salt

    ¾ cup unsalted butter, cold

    1 cup pecans, chopped

    ⅔ cup maple syrup, plus additional for brushing

    ⅓ cup heavy cream

INSTRUCTIONS:

1. Preheat oven to 350°F
2. Line a rimmed baking sheet with parchment paper
3. In a large mixing bowl, whisk together the flour, baking powder, and salt
4. Cut the butter into the flour mixture with 2 forks (I use my fingers), until the mixture resembles coarse meal
5. Stir in the pecans
6. In a small mixing bowl, whisk together the maple syrup and heavy cream until thoroughly combined and smooth
7. Make a well in the flour/butter mixture and pour the maple/cream mixture into it
8. Stir the maple/cream mixture into the flour/butter mixture until the combined mixture begins to become a dough; do not over mix
9. Lightly flour your counter or a cutting board
10. Roll the dough out onto the floured surface until it is about 2 inches thick
11. Using a 3-inch biscuit cutter (I just use a drinking glass that is about 3 inches in diameter), cut rounds from the dough

12. Keep reforming, rolling out and cutting rounds until you have used all the dough
13. Put the rounds about 2 inches apart on the prepared pan
14. Brush the tops of the rounds with maple syrup
15. Transfer the pan with the raw scones onto the center rack of the oven and bake ay 350°F until they are lightly browned (15 to 20 minutes)
16. Serve straight out of the oven with butter

Monte Cristo Sandwich with Maple Syrup Dip

2 servings

INGREDIENTS:

4 slices firm bread, sliced ½-inch thick

¾ cups milk

3 egg yolks

1½ tablespoons light brown sugar

1 tablespoon unsalted butter, melted + ½ tablespoon for cooking

½ tablespoon vanilla extract

⅛ teaspoon Kosher salt

1 teaspoon Dijon mustard

4 ounces ham, sliced

4 ounces Gruyere cheese, shredded

Maple syrup, for serving

INSTRUCTIONS:

1. Very lightly toast the bread (not enough to give it much color, just enough to dry it out)
2. In a medium mixing bowl, whisk together the milk, egg yolks, sugar, melted butter, vanilla extract
3. Pour the milk/egg mixture into a 9-inch x13-inch baking pan
3. Spreading a thin layer (about ¼ teaspoon) of Dijon mustard on each slice of bread
4. On top of the mustard evenly divide the ham between two of the slices of bread
5. On top of the ham, evenly divide the cheese between the two slices of bread
6. On top of the cheese add the final pieces of bread (mustard side down) to form 2 sandwiches
7. Heat a large skillet over medium-low heat and add the ½ tablespoon of butter
8. Put the assembled sandwiches in the milk/egg mixture for 20 seconds
9. Carefully flip the sandwiches over and soak on the other side for an additional 20 seconds

10. Gently put the two sandwiches into the skillet and cook until the bottom bread becomes golden brown (about 3 to 4 minutes)

11. Carefully flip the sandwiches and cook until the second side is golden brown (an additional 3 to 4 minutes).

12. Put each sandwich onto a plate and serve immediately with maple syrup for dipping

Spinach, Quinoa & Pear Salad with Maple Vinaigrette

1 serving

INGREDIENTS:

Salad:

3 ounces baby spinach leaves, washed, drained

½ cup quinoa, rinsed

1 Tablespoon butter

½ cup pecans

1 large ripe pear, washed, stemmed and cored, cut into pieces

1 cup chick peas, rinsed, drained

2 tablespoons fresh parsley, chopped

Kosher salt and freshly ground black pepper, to taste

Maple Vinaigrette:

4 tablespoons extra-virgin olive oil

3 tablespoons white balsamic vinegar

2 tablespoons maple syrup

INSTRUCTIONS:

1. In a small saucepan over medium high heat, combine 1 cup of water, the quinoa and a pinch salt and bring to a boil

2. As soon as the quinoa starts to boil, cover it, reduce heat, and simmer until the water is absorbed (about 20 minutes)

3. Once the water is absorbed, fluff the quinoa with a fork and set it aside

4. Preheat the oven to 350°F

5. Lightly grease a rimmed baking sheet with the butter

6. Put the pecans on to the prepared baking sheet and sprinkle with a little salt

7. Put the baking sheet with the pecans onto the center rack of the oven and bake at 350°F until the pecans are lightly toasted (about 5-10 minutes)

8. Place the spinach in a medium-sized serving bowl and add the quinoa, pear, chick peas and parsley

9. In a small mixing bowl, whisk together the olive oil, vinegar, and maple syrup until thoroughly combined

10. Pour the oil/vinegar/syrup dressing over the spinach and other ingredients in the serving bowl and toss gently to coat

11. Add the toasted pecans to the top of the dressed salad and serve

Maple Curried Red Lentil Soup

4 servings

INGREDIENTS:

2 Tablespoons extra-virgin olive oil

1 medium red onion, diced

1 clove of garlic, minced

2-3 stalks celery, medium dice

1 medium carrot, medium dice

½ sweet potato, small dice

1 teaspoon mustard seeds

½ Tablespoon curry powder

¼ teaspoon ground cinnamon

½ teaspoon ground cumin

¼ teaspoon ground coriander

1 Tablespoon fresh ginger, minced

1 small, red chili, seeds removed, minced

¼ teaspoon Turmeric

1 cup dry, red lentils

5 cups water

1 cup spinach, chopped

2 Tablespoons maple syrup

3 Tablespoons soy sauce

Kosher salt & freshly ground black pepper

fresh parsley, minced

fresh cilantro, minced

INSTRUCTIONS:

1. Heat the oil in a medium-sized pot over medium heat and then add the onions, garlic, celery, carrots, and sweet potato

2. Sauté the onions, garlic, celery, carrots, and sweet potato for 3 minutes

3. Add the mustard seeds, curry powder, cinnamon, cumin, coriander, ginger, chili, and Turmeric to the vegetables and sauté for an additional 2 minutes

4. Stir the Lentils into the pot with the vegetables and spices and then add the water

5. Cook uncovered over medium heat, stirring frequently, until the lentils are soft (about 30 minutes) over medium heat

6. Add the spinach to the pot with the vegetables, spices and lentils and cook a few more minutes until the spinach is wilted

7. Season the soup with maple syrup, soy sauce, salt & pepper

8. Ladle the soup into bowls and then sprinkle the fresh parsley & coriander over the top

Maple and Sriracha Chicken Wings

4 servings

INGREDIENTS:

Sauce:

¾ cup maple syrup

2 Tablespoons Sriracha (or more to taste)

2 Tablespoons ketchup

1 Tablespoons lime juice

1 Tablespoons soy sauce

Chicken Wings:

3½ pounds chicken wings, tips removed, cut at the joint

1 cup all-purpose flour

¼ teaspoon chili powder

1 Tablespoon powdered ginger

1 teaspoon garlic powder

Zest of 1 lime

2 teaspoons Kosher salt

Extra-virgin olive oil

INSTRUCTIONS:

1. In a medium sauce pan sauce pan, stir together the maple syrup, Sriracha, ketchup, lime juice, and soy sauce and, over medium high heat, bring to a boil

2. Once it reaches a boil, let it cook for another 3 to 5 minutes, stirring constantly, until it thickens

3. Once the sauce thickens, remove the pan from the fire and set it aside

4. Line a rimmed baking sheet with parchment paper

5. Preheat the oven to 400°F

6. Mix together the flour, chili powder, garlic powder, ginger powder, lime zest and salt in a sealable 1 gallon plastic bag (shake well to insure all ingredients are thoroughly mixed)

7. About 1 pound at a time, add the chicken wings to the bag with the flour/spice mixture and shake well until the wings are fully coated in the flour mixture

8. Shake the excess flour off the wings and arrange them evenly on the prepared baking sheet

9. Lightly spray the floured/spices wings with a little of the olive oil

10. Transfer the baking sheet to the center rack of the oven and bake at 400°F for 25 minutes

11. After 25 minutes, turn the chicken wings over and bake them on the other side for another 20 minutes

>NOTE: cooking time depends on the size of the wings

12. Once the chicken wings are cooked, coat them thoroughly with the sauce

13. Serve hot with the remaining sauce on the side for dipping

Maple Bacon Party Mix

18 servings

INGREDIENTS:

2 cups Corn Chex™ cereal

2 cups Rice Chex™ cereal

2 cups Wheat Chex™ cereal

1 cup peanuts, salted and roasted

¼ teaspoon cayenne (depending on how spicy you like it)

6 strips bacon, cooked extra crispy and chopped

4 Tablespoons butter, melted

4 Tablespoons maple syrup

1 teaspoon Kosher Salt

INSTRUCTIONS:

1. In a large, microwave-safe mixing bowl, toss together the cereals, peanuts, and cayenne
2. In a small mixing bowl whisk together the butter and maple syrup
3. Pour the maple/butter mixture to the cereal/peanut mixture and stir very well
4. Put the bowl with the cereal/peanut/maple/butter mixture into the microwave and cook on High for 3 minutes, stirring every minute to prevent the sugars from scorching
5. After 3 minutes in the microwave, stir in the bacon and salt. Stir
6. Let it cool before serving

Maple Spiced Candied Nuts

36 servings

INGREDIENTS:

    8 cups (2 pounds) mixed raw nuts

    ¾ cup maple syrup

    3 teaspoons Kosher salt

    ½ teaspoon cayenne pepper (if you like it spicy, double the amount)

    2 teaspoons ground cinnamon

INSTRUCTIONS:

1. Preheat oven to 300°F
2. Line 2 rimmed baking sheets with parchment paper
3. In a large mixing bowl, stir nuts to make sure the different varieties are well distributed
4. In a separate small mixing bowl, whisk together the maple syrup, salt, cayenne and cinnamon
5. Pour the maple/spice mixture over the nuts and stir to coat the nuts evenly
6. Divide the maple/spice/nut mixture between the two prepared baking sheets
7. Transfer the baking sheets to the oven and bake at 300°F for 10 minutes
8. After baking for 10 minutes, stir the coated nuts and then bake until nuts are toasted and coating is sticky (about an additional 10 minutes)
9. When the nuts are cooked, remove the baking pans from the oven and let the nuts cool until coating is dry to the touch (about 5 minutes)
10. Serve while warm or allow the nuts to cool completely and store them in a sealed container

Roasted Lemon-Maple Chicken

6 servings

INGREDIENTS:

    1 (4 pound) roasting chicken

    2 lemons, one quartered and one for juicing

    6 cloves of garlic, peeled and halved

    1 small onion, quartered

    2 tablespoons maple syrup

    3 tablespoons extra-virgin olive oil

    Kosher salt and freshly ground black pepper to taste

INSTRUCTIONS:

1. Preheat oven to 375°F
2. Peel one of the lemons, removing long, thick strips of zest
3. Set zest aside
4. Juice the peeled lemon into a small mixing bowl and whisk in the maple syrup and oil
5. Rub a piece of lemon zest and a halved garlic clove all over the chicken
6. Stuff the lemon zest and garlic that you just rubbed all over the chicken into the cavity of the chicken along with the quartered lemon, onion, and remaining garlic
7. Place the chicken in a roasting pan and brush it with the maple/lemon mixture
8. Sprinkle the maple/lemon brushed chicken with salt and pepper
9. Put the roasting pan with the chicken onto the center rack in the oven and roast for 30 minutes at 375°F
10. After 30 minutes, brush more of the lemon-maple mixture over the chicken and roast for an additional 30 minutes at 375°F

11. After the second 30 minutes (the chicken has been in the oven for 1 hour), brush more of the lemon-maple mixture over the chicken and continue roasting at 375°F until the juices run clear when cut between the thigh and the body (about an additional 20 minutes)

12. When the chicken is thoroughly cooked, remove it from the oven and let it rest for ten minutes before carving and serving

Sesame and Maple Crusted Lamb Chops

4 servings

INGREDIENTS:

    2 Tablespoons maple syrup

    Zest of 1 lemon

    1 Tablespoon fresh ginger, minced

    ½ cup fresh cilantro, chopped

    3 Tablespoons sesame seeds

    Kosher salt and freshly ground black pepper

    8 lamb chops, about 1-inch thick each

    3 Tablespoons extra-virgin olive oil

INSTRUCTIONS:

1. In a small mixing bowl, whisk together the maple syrup, lemon zest, ginger, cilantro, sesame seeds, salt and pepper

2. Evenly coat each of the lamb chops with the maple/lemon/ginger/cilantro/sesame mixture

3. In a large sauté pan over medium heat, heat the oil and brown the chops (about 3 to 4 minutes on each side ... or until they reach your desired level of doneness)

4. Serve immediately

Maple, Ale & Garlic Pork Shoulder

8 servings

INGREDIENTS:

1 (seven pound) pork shoulder, bone-in (sometimes called the "Boston Butt" or the "pork shoulder blade roast")

12 garlic cloves

½ cup extra-virgin olive oil

3 tablespoons Kosher salt

3 tablespoons fennel seeds, toasted

1 teaspoon cayenne pepper

1 teaspoon freshly ground black pepper

¾ cups maple syrup

1 bottle of Belgian Ale (I use the 750ml Matilda from Goose Island Beer Company)

2 teaspoons malt vinegar

INSTRUCTIONS:

1. Preheat oven to 450°F
2. Place the pork shoulder in a roasting pan with the fatty side down
3. Place garlic, oil, salt, fennel seeds, cayenne, and black pepper into the bowl of a food processor and pulse until you have a nice paste
4. Rub ⅓ of the paste over the top of shoulder
5. Transfer the pan with the meat to the lowest rack of the oven and cook at 450°F for 30 minutes
6. Add the maple syrup and vinegar into the remaining garlic/oil/spice paste and pulse the food processor until thoroughly combined
7. Turn the oven down to 225°F
8. Flip the shoulder so the fatty side is up
9. Spread the maple syrup/vinegar/garlic/oil/spice paste over the meat

10. Let the meat cook for 12 hours (or longer), every 3 hours pouring 1/3 of the ale over it and basting with the pan drippings

11. Transfer the meat from the roasting pan to a serving platter and serve

Maple-Cardamom Glazed Salmon

4 servings

INGREDIENTS:

1 (1 pound) salmon filet, de-boned

¼ cup maple syrup

2 teaspoons ground cardamom

1 teaspoon smoked paprika

pinch cayenne pepper

Kosher salt and freshly ground black pepper

INSTRUCTIONS:

1. Preheat the oven to 450°F

2. Lightly grease a rimmed baking sheet

3. In a small mixing bowl, whisk together the maple syrup, cardamom, paprika, cayenne

4. After the maple/spice mixture has been whisked smooth, add salt and pepper to taste

5. Place the salmon, skin side down, on the prepared baking sheet and brush maple/spice mixture evenly over the salmon

6. Transfer the baking sheet with the salmon to top rack of the oven and bake for 10 minutes at 450°F

7. After it has cooked for 10 minutes, brush more glaze onto the salmon let it cook for an additional 5 minutes (or until it is cooked to your preferred level of doneness)

9. When the salmon has finished cooking, transfer it to a serving platter and serve immediately

Maple Garlic Dijon Chicken

4 servings

INGREDIENTS:

4 chicken breasts, boneless, skinless

4 garlic cloves, minced

4 tablespoons maple syrup

4 tablespoons Dijon mustard

1½ teaspoons + 2 tablespoons extra-virgin olive oil

1 Tablespoon parsley flakes

¼ teaspoon cayenne pepper

Kosher salt and freshly ground black pepper (to taste)

INSTRUCTIONS:

1. Preheat oven to 450°F
2. Lightly coat the interior of a rimmed baking sheet with 1½ teaspoons of olive oil
3. In small sauce pan over medium heat, heat 2 tablespoons of olive oil
4. Add the minced garlic to the hot oil and cook, stirring, until the garlic is very lightly browned and tender
5. When the garlic is properly cooked, remove the sauce pan from heat and stir in the maple syrup and mustard
6. Whisk the parsley and cayenne into the garlic/maple/mustard mixture
7. Put the chicken breasts onto the prepared baking sheet and sprinkle with the salt and pepper
8. Cover the chicken with the garlic/maple/mustard mixture
9. Put the baking sheet with the chicken onto the top rack in the oven and bake uncovered at 450°F until there is no pink in the center (about 30 minutes)
7. Once fully cooked, let the chicken rest for 5 to 10 minutes before serving

Maple Vegetable Enchiladas

4 servings

INGREDIENTS:

Enchilada Sauce (if you decide not to use pre-made):

1 Tablespoon extra-virgin olive oil

1 cup onion, diced

2 cloves garlic, minced

½ Tablespoon chili powder

1 teaspoon ground cumin

½ teaspoon dried oregano

1 can (14 ounces) diced tomatoes

1 teaspoon maple syrup

⅓ cup water (or as needed)

Kosher salt to taste

Enchiladas:

3 Tablespoons extra-virgin olive oil, divided

3 cups zucchini, medium dice

3 cups sweet potato, medium dice

1 can (16 ounces) black beans, drained

2 green onions, chopped

1½ cups enchilada sauce (as above)

¾ cup Cheddar cheese, shredded

10 white or yellow corn tortillas

INSTRUCTIONS:

Enchilada Sauce:

1. In a medium-sized skillet on medium high heat, heat the olive oil

2. Add the onion to the hot oil and sauté for 3 minutes

3. Add garlic to the onions and continue cooking until the onions are translucent (about 5 minutes)

4. Stir the chili powder, cumin, oregano, tomatoes, and maple syrup in with the onions and garlic

5. Add salt (to taste) to the onion/garlic/maple/spice mixture

6. Transfer the onion/garlic/maple/spice mixture to a food processor, and process until the mixture until it is smooth ... adding water to adjust the consistency to your preferred level

7. Set aside the sauce until you need it

Enchiladas:

1. Preheat the oven to 375°F

2. Line 2 rimmed baking sheets with foil

3. In a large mixing bowl, toss the zucchini with 1½ Tablespoons of the olive oil, place it on one of the prepared baking sheet and season it with salt and pepper

4. In the same mixing bowl you used for the zucchini, toss the sweet potato with the remaining 1½ Tablespoons of oil, place it on the other prepared baking sheet and season it with salt and pepper

5. Place both sheets in the oven roast the vegetables at 375°F until they're golden and tender (about 25 minutes)

   NOTE: The zucchini may be done first; if so, remove that tray sooner than the potatoes

6. Lower the oven temperature to 350°F

7. In the large mixing bowl, toss the roasted zucchini and potatoes together with the black beans and the green onion ... add a little salt and/or pepper if needed

8. Spread ½ cup of the enchilada sauce evenly over the bottom of a 9-inch x13-inch casserole dish.

9. Fill each tortilla with about ⅓ cup of the vegetable mixture

10. Put about a Tablespoon of the cheese on top of the vegetables

11. Roll each of the tortilla up and place them, seam down, in the casserole dish until all of the tortillas have been used and the dish is packed

12. Pour the remaining enchilada sauce over the top of the tortillas and evenly sprinkle the remaining cheese over the top

13. Transfer the filled baking dish to the middle rack of the oven and bake at 350°F until the tortillas are just getting crispy and the sauce is dark (about 20 minutes)

14. Once the enchiladas are cooked, serve immediately

Maple Mustard Pork Tenderloin

6 servings

INGREDIENTS:

2 tablespoons Dijon mustard

1 Tablespoon extra-virgin olive oil

3 large cloves garlic, minced

1 cup maple syrup

1 pork tenderloin (1 - 1½ pounds)

Kosher salt and freshly ground black pepper

1 Tablespoon butter

¼ cup flat leaf parsley, roughly chopped

INSTRUCTIONS:

1. In a small mixing bowl, whisk together the mustard, oil, garlic, maple syrup, salt, pepper
2. Put the tenderloin in 1-gallon, resealable plastic bag and pour the mustard/oil/garlic/maple mixture over the port in the bag
3. Seal the plastic bag and move the ingredients around to make sure the tenderloin is thoroughly coated and then put the bag into the fridge to marinate overnight (or minimum of 8 hours).
4. Preheat grill to medium-low heat
5. Remove the tenderloin from the marinade and set it aside
6. Pour the remaining marinade into a small saucepan, and cook over medium-low heat for 5 minutes to reduce
7. Spray or brush the grill grating with oil to prevent sticking
8. Put the tenderloin on the oiled grate and brown each side for 2 minutes
9. Grill the pork for 15-20 minutes, basting every 5 minutes with the reduced marinade, until the interior of tenderloin is pink (internal temperature of 160°)

10. When the tenderloin is properly cooked, transfer it from the grill to a cutting board and cover with tin foil to rest for 10 minutes

11. Turn the heat under the saucepan containing the marinade to low and stir in the butter

12. Once the meat has rested, slice it in thick slices, spoon the remaining hot marinade over it, garnish it with the parsley and serve immediately

Slow Cooker Maple Ham

10 servings

INGREDIENTS:

    1 bone-in spiral-cut ham (7-8 pounds)

    1 cup dark brown sugar

    ½ cup maple syrup

    2 cups pineapple juice

INSTRUCTIONS:

Use a 6-7 quart slow cooker.

1. Unwrap the ham, and discard flavor packet
2. Place the ham, flat-side down, into the stoneware pot of the slow cooker (suggest a 6 quart or larger capacity)
3. Rub the brown sugar on all sides of the ham
4. Pour on the maple syrup and then the pineapple juice
5. Place the cover on the slow cooker, set the level to Low and cook for 6 hours
6. After the ham has cooked for 6 hours, baste it with the juice that has collected in the stoneware pot
7. After basting the ham, cook it on Low for an additional hour
8. When the ham is properly cooked, remove it from the stoneware pot carefully and set it on a cutting board
9. Let the meat rest on the cutting board for 15 minutes before carving and serving

Maple Mashed Sweet Potatoes

12 servings

INGREDIENTS:

4 pounds medium sweet potatoes, washed (suggest Garnet, which is often mis-labeled as a yam)

6 Tablespoons (¾ stick) unsalted butter, melted

½ cup heavy cream, at room temperature

2 Tablespoons maple syrup

½ teaspoon Kosher salt, plus more as needed

¼ teaspoon freshly ground black pepper, plus more as needed

INSTRUCTIONS:

1. Preheat the oven to 375°F
2. Line a rimmed baking sheet with foil
3. Put the sweet potatoes on the prepared baking sheet and put the baking sheet with the potatoes onto the middle rack of the oven and bake at 375°F until knife-tender (45 - 60 minutes)
4. When the potatoes are fully cooked, transfer the baking sheet with the potatoes from the oven to on a wire rack to cool until, although still warm, they can be handled (about 20 minutes)
5. When cool enough to handle, cut the sweet potatoes in half lengthwise and scrape the flesh out with a spoon into a large mixing bowl (discard the skins)
6. Use a potato masher to mash the cooked potatoes in the mixing bowl until they are smooth
7. Add the butter, cream, and maple syrup and stir until the ingredients are combined
8. Taste, the potato/butter/cream/maple mixture, season with additional salt and pepper to taste, and stir again to mix in the salt and pepper
9. Serve immediately

Maple Almond Squares

12 servings

INGREDIENTS:

Crust:

1¼ cups all-purpose flour

⅓ cup light brown sugar

½ cup butter, softened

Topping:

1 cup maple syrup

½ cup light brown sugar

2 large eggs, beaten well

2 tablespoons butter, melted

1 ½ teaspoons vanilla

2 tablespoons all-purpose flour

¼ teaspoon Kosher salt

1 cup chopped almonds, divided

INSTRUCTIONS:

1. Preheat the oven to 375°F

2. Greased an 8-inch square baking dish

3. In a medium-sized mixing bowl, sift together flour and sugar

4. Cut the butter into the flour/sugar mix and blend until the mixture resembles coarse meal

5. Press the butter/flour/sugar mixture into the bottom of the prepared baking dish

6. Put the filled baking dish onto the middle rack of the oven and bake at 375°F for 15 minutes

7. After baking for 15 minutes, remove the baking dish with the crust from the oven and allow it to cool

8. Reduce the oven temperature to 350°F

8. In a medium-sized mixing bowl, whisk together the maple syrup and sugar

9. Whisk the eggs into the maple/sugar mixture

10. Stir the butter, vanilla, flour, salt and ¾ cup of the almonds, mixing well until thoroughly mixed

11. Pour the maple/sugar/egg/butter/vanilla/four mixture evenly onto the crust in the baking dish

12. Sprinkle the remaining ¼ cup of almonds on top of the ingredients in the baking dish

13. Return the baking dish to the oven and bake at 350°F until slightly browned and bubbly (25-30 minutes)

14. Once finished cooking, remove the baking dish from the oven and set it on a cooling rack to cool completely in the baking dish

15. Once completely cooled, refrigerate for a minimum of 2 hours

15. Once chilled, cut into squares and serve

Maple Apple Pie

8 servings

INGREDIENTS:

Crust:

2 cups all-purpose flour

½ teaspoon Kosher salt

⅔ cup shortening

6 to 7 Tablespoons cold water

Filling:

8 apples peeled, cored & cut into wedges (suggest a variety: Rome, Cortland, Granny Smith)

1 cup Maple Syrup

¾ cup all-purpose flour

½ teaspoon ground cinnamon

½ teaspoon ground nutmeg

¼ teaspoon Kosher Salt

1½ Tablespoons unsalted butter, cut into small pieces

1 Tablespoon heavy whipping cream (as needed)

1½ Tablespoons Maple Sugar

INSTRUCTIONS:

1. Preheat oven 375°F

Crust:

2. In a large mixing bowl, sift together the flour and salt

3. Using a pastry blender cut in the shortening until it is separated into pea-sized pieces throughout the dough

4. Sprinkle the water over the flour/shortening mixture and blend thoroughly (suggestion: use your hands)

5. Divide the dough into 2 parts: about ⅔ for the bottom crust and about ⅓ for the top

6. Roll out the dough for the bottom crust into a 14-inch round; roll out the dough for the top crust into an 11-inch round

7. Place the bottom crust into a 9-inch pie dish, allowing the excess to hang over the sides

Filling:

8. In large mixing bowl toss together the apples, flour, maple syrup, cinnamon, nutmeg & salt; toss until coated

9. Scrape the apple/flour/maple/spice mixture to the dough-lined pie dish

10. Sprinkle the pieces of butter on top of the apple/flour/maple/spice mixture

11. Place top portion of dough onto pie

12. Crimp the edge as desired

13. Create vents by inserting the knife in several places through top crust

14. Brush the top of crust of the pie with heavy cream and then sprinkle the maple sugar on top of that

15. Put the pie on the middle rack of the oven and bake at Heat oven 375°F until the filling is bubbly and top crust is golden brown (about 1 - 1½ hours)

16. Once the pie is fully cooked, remove it from the oven and allow it to cool at least 2 hours before serving

Peach Crisp with Maple Cream Sauce

8 Servings

INGREDIENTS:

    6 fresh peaches, peeled, sliced

    1 cup all-purpose flour

    ½ cup granulated white sugar

    ½ cup light brown sugar, firmly packed

    ½ teaspoon ground cinnamon

    ½ teaspoon ground nutmeg

    ¼ teaspoon kosher salt

    1 stick butter (½ cup)

    zest of ½ fresh lemon

    juice of ½ fresh lemon

    7 tablespoons maple syrup, divided

    1½ cup whipping cream

    3 tablespoons light corn syrup

INSTRUCTIONS:

1. Preheat oven to 350°F

2. Lightly grease a 9-inch square baking dish

3. In a medium-sized mixing bowl, combine the flour, white sugar, brown sugar, cinnamon, nutmeg and salt until it is coarsely mixed

4. Cut the butter into small pieces and cut it in to the flour/sugar/spice mixture until evenly mixed

5. In a large mixing bowl, toss together the peaches with the lemon zest, lemon juice, and 2 tablespoons of the maple syrup to peaches

6. Pour peach mixture into the prepared baking dish and top small pan (8" or 9" square) and top evenly with the butter/flour/sugar/spice mixture co

7. Cover the filled baking dish with foil, put it on the middle rack of the oven and bake at 350°F for 15 minutes
8. After 15 minutes of baking, remove foil and bake until the top is crisp and brown (about an additional 20-30 minutes)
9. In a saucepan over medium heat, add the whipping cream, the remaining 5 tablespoons of maple syrup, and the corn syrup and until thickened and reduced by about ⅓ (about 15 minutes)
10. Once the ingredients have been reduced by ⅓, place the saucepan into a small bowl of ice and stir to cool and thicken the sauce
11. Serve the peach crisp warm, drizzled with the maple/cream sauce

Bourbon Maple Bacon and Pecan Cookies

24 servings

INGREDIENTS:

1 cup butter, softened

1½ cups granulated white sugar

2 eggs

1 teaspoon maple extract

2 tablespoons bourbon whiskey

2¼ cups all-purpose flour

1 teaspoon Kosher salt

1 teaspoon baking soda

2 cups pecan pieces

½ cup crispy bacon pieces (about 8 ounces of bacon cooked to crispy and chopped)

INSTRUCTIONS:

1. Preheat the oven to 350°F
2. Line 2 rimmed baking sheets with parchment paper
3. In a large mixing bowl, beat together the butter and sugar until light and fluffy (about 4 minutes)
4. Add the eggs to the butter/sugar mixture and combine well
5. Add the maple extract and the bourbon and combine thoroughly
6. In a separate large mixing bowl, sift together the flour, salt and baking soda
7. Add half the flour mixture to the maple/bourbon/butter/sugar mixture and mix to moisten the dry ingredients
8. Add the remaining half the flour mixture to the maple/bourbon/butter/sugar/flour mixture and mix until you have a sticky dough
9. Add the pecans and bacon to the dough and mix until the nuts and bacon are evenly distributed

10. Put Tablespoon-sized pieces of the cookie dough onto the prepared baking sheets, leaving about 3 inches between the dough pieces

11. Put the baking sheets with the cookie dough pieces into the oven and bake at 350°F until the cookies start to brown around the edges (about 12 minutes)

12. Once properly cooked, remove the baking sheets from the oven and let the cookies cool for 10 minutes on the baking sheet before transferring them to a cooling rack

13. Serve when the cookies have fully cooled

Maple Syrup Gingerbread Cookies

24 servings

INGREDIENTS:

1 cup pure maple syrup

2 tablespoons butter

¼ teaspoon ground ginger

⅛ teaspoon ground cloves

⅛ teaspoon ground cinnamon

2⅓ cup all-purpose flour, divided

1 egg yolk

1 teaspoon baking powder, dissolved in boiling water

Optional Garnish: maple butter, decorative icing, maple sugar, mini candies

INSTRUCTIONS:

1. Preheat the oven to 350°F
2. Line a rimmed baking sheet with parchment paper
3. In a small sauce pan over low heat, combine and heat the maple syrup and butter
4. Once the maple/butter mixture is well combined and warm, whisk in the ginger, cloves and cinnamon
5. Once the spices have been thoroughly mixed into the maple/butter mixture, remove the sauce pan from the heat and set it aside to cool
6. Into a large mixing bowl, sift 1½ cups of the flour and then make a "well" in the center of the flour
7. Pour the cooled maple/butter/spice mixture, the egg yolk and the dissolved baking powder into the well in the flour in the mixing bowl

8. Knead the flour/egg/maple/butter/spice mixture; and as you knead, add the remaining flour a bit at a time until you have a firm dough that doesn't stick to the sides of the bowl

9. When the dough is the correct consistency, transfer it from the bowl to a floured surface, and, using a rolling-pin, roll it out to ¼-inch thick

10. Use a cookie cutter to cut the rolled out dough into shapes (or use a variety cookie cutters to get a number of different shapes) and place the dough shapes onto the prepared baking sheet leaving about 2-inches space between them

11. Put the filled baking sheet on to the top rack in the oven and bake at 350°F until the cookies are slightly golden (about 10 minutes)

12. Once the cookies are properly cooked, remove them from the oven and allow them to cool on the baking sheet for 5 minutes before transferring them to a rack to cool completely

13. When the cookies are completely cool, either serve them, store them in an airtight container or use maple butter, decorative icing, maple sugar, mini candies to decorate them

Maple Panna Cotta

Serves 6

INGREDIENTS:

    2 teaspoons unflavored gelatin

    2 Tablespoons warm water

    1 cup heavy whipping cream

    1 cup mascarpone cheese, room temperature

    1 cup maple syrup

    1 tablespoon dark rum

    whipped cream for garnish

    Optional Garnish: maple sugar candies

INSTRUCTIONS:

1. In a large oven proof bowl, pour in the water and sprinkle the gelatin over it
2. Let the water with the gelatin sprinkled over it sit for 10 minutes
3. Add the cream, mascarpone and maple syrup to the water & gelatin, set the bowl over a pan of simmering water, and whisk the mixture until it is smooth and warmed through and the gelatin is completely incorporated
4. Divide the mixture evenly between 6 martini glasses
5. Individually cover each glass with plastic wrap, making sure that the wrap does not touch the contents of the glass and put the glasses in the fridge
6. Refrigerate the filled & covered martini glasses for a minimum of 12 hours, before serving
7. Just before serving, top with each glass with a dollop of whipped cream (and a maple sugar candy if desired)

Sweet & Spicy Nutty Maple Bites

6 servings

INGREDIENTS:

1 ounce almonds, chopped

1 ounce roasted unsalted peanuts, chopped

2 Tablespoons maple syrup, divided

¼ teaspoon chili powder

¼ teaspoon cayenne

A pinch of granulated white sugar

A pinch of Kosher salt

INSTRUCTIONS:

1. Preheat the oven to 350°F
2. Line a rimmed baking sheet with parchment paper
3. In a medium-sized mixing bowl, combine the chopped nuts, 1Tablespoon of the maple syrup, the chili powder and the cayenne and mix thoroughly
4. Once mixed, divide the nut/maple/spice mixture into 6 equal parts and distribute them evenly on the prepared baking sheet, slightly flattening out each one
5. Drizzle the remaining maple syrup evenly over each piece of the nut/maple/spice mixture on the baking sheet
6. Put the baking sheet with the nut/maple/spice mixture into the oven and bake at 350°F for ten minutes.
7. Once cooked, remove the baking sheet from the oven and sprinkle a tiny bit of sugar and salt over the tops of each of the "bites"
8. Let the "bites" cool on the baking sheet
9. Once the "bites" have cooled, transfer them to a serving plate

NOTE: if the "bites" are difficult to remove from the parchment paper, but the baking sheet in the fridge for an hour and try again

Nutmeg-Maple Cream Pie

8 servings

INGREDIENTS:

    1 9-inch pie crust in pan

    ¾ cup maple syrup

    2¼ cups heavy cream

    4 egg yolks

    1 egg

    ¼ teaspoon Kosher salt

    1 teaspoon freshly grated nutmeg

    1 teaspoon vanilla extract

INSTRUCTIONS:

1. Preheat the oven to 350°F

2. Place parchment paper over the pie crust and then cover the parchment paper with pie weights
NOTE: Dried beans can be used in lieu of pie weights to keep the bottom of the pie level and even during cooking

3. Put the pie shell (in the pan) with the weights in the oven and bake t 350°F until it begins to set (about 10-12 minutes)

4. After 10 minutes or so (the shell is beginning to set), remove the parchment paper and weights and bake at 350°F until it turns golden (about an additional 15-18 minutes)

5. When the shell is golden, remove the pan from the oven and set on a wire rack to cool

6. Lower the oven temperature to 300°F

7. In a medium-sized sauce pan over medium-high heat, reduce the maple syrup by a quarter (about 6 minutes)

8. Stir the cream into the reduced maple syrup and bring the maple/cream mixture to a simmer

9. As soon as the maple/cream mixture starts to simmer, remove it from the heat and set it aside to cool

10. In a medium-sized mixing bowl, whisk together the egg yolks and the whole egg

11. Once the egg yolks and whole egg are well combined, continue to whisk and slowly add maple/cream mixture to eggs

12. When the egg/maple/cream mixture is thoroughly combined, strain mixture through a fine-mesh sieve into a clean bowl (I use a large glass measuring cup with a spout)

13. Stir the salt, nutmeg and vanilla into the strained egg/maple/cream mixture

14. Pour the egg/maple/cream/spice mixture into the cooked pie shell

15. Transfer the filled pie crust onto the middle rack of the oven and bake at 300°F until pie is firm to touch but jiggles slightly when moved (about 1 hour)

16. When the pie has been properly cooked, remove it from the oven and let cool to room temperature before serving

Maple Syrup Raisin Bread

1 loaf/12 servings

INGREDIENTS:

　　2 cups all-purpose flour

　　4 teaspoons baking powder

　　1 teaspoon Kosher salt

　　¾ cup milk

　　½ cup maple syrup

　　1 egg, beaten

　　1 cup raisins

INSTRUCTIONS:

1. Preheat oven to 350°F

2. Grease and flour a 9-inch x 5-inch loaf pan

3. In a large mixing bowl, sift together the flour, baking powder, and salt

4. Stir the milk, maple syrup, and egg into the flour mixture and mix well until thoroughly combined

5. Stir the raisins into the milk/maple/egg/flour mixture

6. Scrape the dough into the prepared loaf pan

7. Put the dough-filled loaf pan onto the center rack of the oven and bake at 350° until the top is well browned (about 50 - 60 minutes)

8. When the bread is properly cooked, remove it from the oven and cool in the pan for 10 minutes

9. After cooling in the pan, turn the loaf out onto a cooling rack

10. Allow the bread to cool completely before slicing and serving

Sweet Potato Maple Beer Bread

1 loaf/12 servings

INGREDIENTS:

½ cup mashed sweet potato*

2 tablespoons canola oil

2 tablespoons medium molasses

⅓ cup maple syrup

1 teaspoon ground cinnamon

½ teaspoon ground nutmeg

½ teaspoon ground cloves

½ teaspoon Kosher salt

2½ cups all-purpose flour

1 tablespoon baking powder

12 ounces beer (I use Yuengling Lager)

INSTRUCTIONS:

1. Preheat oven to 375°F
2. Grease and flour a 9-inch x 5-inch loaf pan
3. In a large mixing bowl, whisk together the sweet potato, oil, molasses, maple syrup, cinnamon, nutmeg, cloves and salt
4. Stir the flour and baking powder into the potato/maple/spice mixture
5. Pour the beer over the top of the flour/ potato/maple/spice mixture

   NOTE: the beer will bubble and foam

6. Stir the beer into the flour/ potato/maple/spice mixture until combined and no white bits remain at bottom of bowl

   NOTE: the batter will be dense and relatively wet

7. Scrape the batter into prepared pan

8. Put the batter-filled loaf pan onto the middle shelf of the oven and bake it at 375°F until top is domed, firm and set, and a toothpick inserted in the center comes out clean (about 40 minutes)

9. When the bread is fully cooked, remove it from the oven and allow it to cool in the pan for 15 minutes before out turning onto a cooling rack

10. Allow the bread to cool fully before slicing and serving

*Cook a small to medium-sized sweet potato in a microwave on high for 7 minutes, peel it and mash it with a fork

Maple-Lemon Zucchini Bread

1 loaf/12 servings

INGREDIENTS:

    3 eggs

    1 cup maple syrup

    ½ cup canola oil

    1 teaspoon vanilla extract

    zest of 1 lemon, finely grated

    1½ cups grated zucchini

    1½ cups unbleached or all-purpose flour

    1 cup whole-wheat flour

    1 tablespoon baking powder

    ½ teaspoon Kosher salt

INSTRUCTIONS:

1. Preheat oven to 350°F
2. Grease a 5-inch x 9-inch loaf pan
3. In a large mixing bowl, beat the eggs with an electric mixer for 2 minutes
4. Continue beating the eggs with the mixer while gradually adding the maple syrup, oil, vanilla, and lemon zest until well mixed in
5. With a large spoon, stir in the zucchini into the egg/maple/oil/vanilla/lemon mixture
6. In a large mixing bowl, sift together the unbleached and wheat flours, baking powder, and salt
7. Make a well in the center of the flour mixture
8. Pour the zucchini mixture into the well in the flour mixture and stir just until it is smooth
9. Scrape the zucchini/flour mixture into the prepared loaf pan
10. Put the dough-filled loaf pan onto the center rack of the oven and bake at 350°F, until a knife inserted into the center comes out clean (about 50 to 60 minutes)

11. When the bread is properly cooked, remove it from the oven and cool in the pan for 5 to 10 minutes

12. After cooling in the pan, turn the loaf out onto a cooling rack

13. Allow the bread to cool completely before slicing and serving

Sour Cream-Maple Bread

1 loaf/12 servings

INGREDIENTS:

    1¾ cups all-purpose flour

    2 teaspoon baking powder

    1 teaspoon baking soda

    ½ teaspoon Kosher salt

    8 Tablespoons (1 stick) unsalted butter, room temperature

    ¾ cup maple syrup

    1 cup sour cream

    1 egg

    ½ cup chopped pecans

INSTRUCTIONS:

1. Preheat an oven to 350°F
2. Grease and flour a 1-pound loaf pan
3. In a medium-sized mixing bowl, sift together the flour, baking powder, baking soda and salt
4. In a large bowl, beat the butter until it is smooth
5. Once the butter is smooth, slowly whisk in the maple syrup
6. When the butter and maple syrup are thoroughly combined, whisk in the sour cream and egg
7. When the butter/maple/sour cream mixture is thoroughly blended, stir in the pecans until evenly distributed
8. Add the flour mixture to the butter/maple/sour cream/pecan mixture and stir until just blended
9. Scrape the batter into the prepared loaf pan transfer the filled loaf pan to the oven and bake at 350°F until a toothpick inserted into the center of the loaf comes out clean (about 50 to 60 minutes)
10. When the bread is properly cooked, let it cool in the pan, on a wire rack, for 5 minutes
11. After 5 minutes of cooling in the pan, turn the loaf out onto the rack to let cool completely

Maple White Bread

1 loaf/12 servings

INGREDIENTS:

  1 cup milk

  ¼ cup maple syrup

  4 tablespoons sweet butter

  1 teaspoon Kosher salt

  1 package active dry yeast

  ¼ cup warm water (about 110°F)

  1 teaspoon granulated white sugar or maple sugar

  1 egg beaten

  4 cups (approximately) unbleached all-purpose flour

INSTRUCTIONS:

1. In a medium-sized sauce pan over high heat, stir together the milk, maple syrup, butter and salt
2. Heat the milk/maple/butter mixture until it scalds and then let it cool down to a lukewarm temperature
3. In a small mixing bowl, dissolve the yeast in the warm water and then stir in the sugar
4. Set the yeast/water/sugar mixture aside until it becomes "frothy" (about 5 minutes)
5. In a large mixing bowl, stir together the milk/maple/butter mixture with the egg
6. Stir 2 cups of the flour into the egg/milk/maple/butter and then continue to add flour, about half a cup at a time, until a ball of dough forms
7. Once the dough has properly formed, turn it out onto a floured surface and knead it until the dough is smooth and elastic (about 8 minutes)
NOTE: as you knead the dough, add extra flour as necessary to keep the dough from sticking
8. Lightly oil a medium to large mixing bowl and put the dough in it; turning the dough to get oil on all sides

9. Cover the bowl with a clean kitchen towel and set it aside to rise until doubled (about 1 hour)

10. Grease a 9-inch x 5-inch x 3-inch baking pan

11. After the dough has risen to double its original size, punch it down dough, turn it onto a lightly floured surface, and knead it for another 2 minutes

12. After kneading it, roll the dough into a rectangle about 9-inches by 12-inches and then roll the rectangle tightly (like a jellyroll), starting from the narrow side

13. After tightly rolling the dough, pinch closed the seam and the ends

14. Fit the dough, seam side down, into the prepared baking pan

15. Cover the dough-filled baking pan with a clean kitchen towel and set it in a warm place to rise until doubled (about 45 minutes)

16. Preheat oven to 350°F

17. Once the dough in the baking pan as doubled in sized, put the dough-filled baking pan on the center rack of the oven and bake at 350°F until the top is well browned (about 45 minutes)

18. When the bread is finished cooking, remove it from the baking pan and set it on a cooling rack

19. Allow the bread to cool completely before slicing

Maple Syrup Corn Bread

12 servings

INGREDIENTS:

¾ cup all-purpose flour

½ cup whole wheat flour

1 cup corn meal

2 teaspoons baking powder

1 teaspoon Kosher salt

1 egg

¾ cup milk

½ cup maple syrup

3 tablespoons butter, melted

INSTRUCTIONS:

1. Preheat an oven to 400°F
2. Grease a 9-inch square baking pan
3. In a large mixing bowl, sift together both flours, the cornmeal, baking powder and salt
4. In a small mixing bowl, whisk together the egg, milk, maple syrup and butter
5. Stir the egg/milk/maple/butter mixture into the flour/cornmeal mixture until it is just moistened
6. Pour the batter into the prepared baking pan
7. Put the filled baking pan onto the center shelf of the oven and bake at 400°F until a toothpick inserted near the center comes out clean (15-20 minutes)
8. When the corn bread is finished cooking serve immediately

The Bubbly Maple Leaf

1 serving

INGREDIENTS:

    1 ounce Scotch whiskey

    1 ounce maple syrup

    ½ ounce lemon juice

    3 ounces sparkling wine (suggest Prosecco)

INSTRUCTIONS:

1. Pour the Scotch, maple syrup and lemon juice into a cocktail shaker filled with ice
2. Shake until well mixed and very cold (about 25 seconds)
3. Strain into a Champagne flute
4. Top with the sparkling wine

The Maple Bourbon Twist

1 serving

INGREDIENTS:

    1 ounce bourbon whiskey

    ¾ ounce maple syrup

    ¾ ounce lemon juice, fresh squeezed

    ½ ounce apple brandy

INSTRUCTIONS:

1. Pour all the ingredients into a cocktail shaker filled with ice
2. Shake until well mixed (about 15 seconds)
3. Strain into a chilled cocktail glass.

Rum & Maple with Lime

1 serving

INGREDIENTS:
    1 teaspoon maple syrup
    1 ½ ounce dark rum
    1 ounce fresh lime juice

INSTRUCTIONS:
1. Pour all the ingredients into a cocktail shaker filled with ice
2. Shake until well mixed (about 15 seconds)
3. Strain into a cocktail glass

BONUS RECIPE

This recipe comes from my first volume of maple syrup recipes *The Maple Syrup Cookbook - 40 Easy, Delicious, & Healthy Maple Syrup Recipes for Breakfast Lunch & Dinner*:

Mom's Maple Chewies
(Cookies)

24 servings

INGREDIENTS:

    2 cups all-purpose flour

    ½ teaspoon baking soda

    ½ teaspoon ground ginger

    ¼ teaspoon cinnamon

    ½ teaspoon Kosher salt

    1 stick unsalted butter, at room temperature

    1 cup dark brown sugar

    1 teaspoon vanilla extract

    1 egg

    ¾ cup maple syrup

INSTRUCTIONS:

1. In a medium-sized mixing bowl, sift together the flour, baking soda, ginger, cinnamon, and salt.
2. In a large mixing bowl, beat together the butter and sugar until light and fluffy (about 4 minutes)
3. Add the vanilla and egg to the butter/sugar mixture and beat until well combined
4. Add the maple syrup to the vanilla/egg/butter/sugar mixture and beat until well combined
5. Add half the flour/spice mixture to the maple/vanilla/egg/butter/sugar mixture and stir until it is until just incorporated

6. Add the remaining half of the flour and, again, stir until just incorporated

7. Use plastic wrap to cover bowl and put it in the fridge for 1 hour

8. Preheat the oven to 350°F

9. Line two rimmed baking sheets with parchment paper

10. Remove the dough from the fridge and place it, one tablespoon at a time, on the prepared baking sheets

      NOTE: Keep the cookies three inches apart

11. Put the baking sheets with the cookie dough into the oven and bake at 350°F until the cookies turn golden around the edges (about 10 minutes)

12. Once properly cooked, remove the baking sheets from the oven and let the cookies cool for 10 minutes on the sheets until transferring them to a cooling rack

13. Serve warm or wait for them to be fully cooled

About the Author

Jean LeGrand is unsure whether he cooks because he likes to eat or that he eats because he likes to cook.

"Actually," he says, "I cook for a number of reasons beyond just paying the bills." Here are some of the reasons he offers:

"I think cooking is an art, a form of self-expression, so I cook to create something new."

" I like how cooking brings family and friends together."

"I enjoy the creative process and get a kick out of watching my friends and family enjoy my creations."

"The exploration aspect of cooking -- new tastes and new techniques -- is very exciting."

"I'm good at it, so I get a great feeling of satisfaction and pride when I make a dish that brings compliments ... the biggest one being when things start to get quiet because everybody is enjoying the food experience so much that they forget to talk."

LeGrand writes recipe books because "I like the fact that I can take all the enjoyment I get from cooking and extend it beyond my circle of family and friends. It makes me happy that I'm helping people enjoy both the cooking and eating sides of great food."

Recipe Books by Best Selling Author Jean LeGrand include:

The Maple Syrup Cookbook Volume 2 -   Romantic Treats - Top Paleo Diet Recipes
Fruit Infused Water Recipes - FrankenFood Recipes #1 - FrankenFood Recipes #2
Delicious & Healthy Paleo Recipes - Easter Brunch - Easter Dinner
Mother's Day Recipes - Irish Treats - Irish Dinner - Irish Drinks

Can I Ask a Favor?

Thank you so much for reading my book. I hope you really liked it.

As you probably know, many people look at the reviews on Amazon before they decide to purchase a book.

If you liked the book, **could you please take a minute** to leave a review with your feedback?

Just go to Amazon.com, look up *Maple Cookbook - LeGrand*, go to the book's page) and scroll down until you see the orange "Write a customer review button", click it and write a few words about why you like the book.

 A couple of minutes is all I'm asking for, and it would mean the world to me.

Thank you so much,

Jean